W9-AZG-324

REVIEW COPY
COURTESY OF
ENSLOW PUBLISHERS, INC

A. Kim

Amelia Earhart

Meet the Pilot

Carin T. Ford

Enslow Publishers, Inc.

40 Industrial Road   PO Box 38
Box 398   Aldershot
Berkeley Heights, NJ 07922   Hants GU12 6BP
USA   UK

http://www.enslow.com

Copyright © 2002 by Enslow Publishers, Inc.

All rights reserved.

No part of this book may be reproduced by any means without the written permission of the publisher.

Library of Congress Cataloging-in-Publication Data

Ford, Carin T.
    Amelia Earhart : meet the pilot / Carin T. Ford.
        p. cm. — (Meeting famous people)
    Includes index.
    Summary: A biography of the first woman pilot to cross the Atlantic Ocean and to fly alone across the United States, as well as the first pilot to fly alone across the Pacific Ocean.
    ISBN 0-7660-2003-7 (hardcover)
    1. Earhart, Amelia, 1897–1937—Juvenile literature. 2. Women air pilots—United States—Biography—Juvenile literature. 3. Air pilots—United States—Biography—Juvenile literature. [1. Earhart, Amelia, 1897–1937. 2. Air pilots. 3. Women—Biography.] I. Title. II. Series.
    TL540.E3 F67   2002
    629.13'092—dc21

                                                                                    2002001632

Printed in the United States of America

10 9 8 7 6 5 4 3 2 1

To Our Readers
We have done our best to make sure all Internet Addresses in this book were active and appropriate when we went to press. However, the author and the publisher have no control over and assume no liability for the material available on those Internet sites or on other Web sites they may link to. Any comments or suggestions can be sent by e-mail to comments@enslow.com or to the address on the back cover.

Every effort has been made to locate all copyright holders of material used in this book. If any errors or omissions have occurred, corrections will be made in future editions of this book.

Illustration Credits: AP/Wide World Photos, p. 4 (plane); © 1999 Artville, LLC, pp. 22(T), 26–27(T); Library of Congress, pp. 3, 4 (portrait), 8(T), 12, 13, 14, 16, 18(B), 20, 21, 22(B), 23, 25, 27(B); Schlesinger Library, Radcliffe Institute, Harvard University, pp. 6, 7, 8(B), 10, 11, 17, 28(B).

Cover Illustration: Library of Congress

Table of Contents

Amelia Earhart became a famous pilot.

Chapter 1

Childhood Adventures

 melia Mary Earhart was born in Atchison, Kansas, on July 24, 1897. This was a time when girls were supposed to be quiet and polite. They were supposed to wear long dresses and play with dolls.

But not Amelia.

She and her younger sister, Muriel, liked to wear baggy pants that came down to their knees. In pants, Amelia was free to jump fences and play football and basketball. She could go fishing, ride horses, and shoot her gun at the rats in the barn.

"I am sure I was a horrid little girl," Amelia said. She certainly was an adventurous girl.

When Amelia was seven, she decided to build a roller coaster. Her uncle helped. They leaned planks of wood against the roof of her father's toolshed. Amelia rubbed grease on the planks to make them slippery. Next she pulled a wooden crate up to the roof. This would be the car for her roller coaster. Amelia climbed into the crate.

Zoom! The car raced down the planks. Then it skidded off the track. Amelia was dumped onto the ground. But she was not scared. She was thrilled.

Six-year-old Amelia dressed up for this picture— but she was happier playing outside in pants.

"It's just like flying!" Amelia told her sister.

Amelia's parents, Amy and Edwin Earhart, wanted their daughters to try new things and to explore the world. Amelia often took nature walks with her mother. She collected worms, moths, and toads. She was interested in everything.

Amelia's favorite hobby was reading. Her grandfather had a large library, and she loved reading the stories in his books. But Amelia was angry that the books she read—even the children's books—were always about boys. It was not fair that girls never had exciting adventures.

Amelia had to be content with her dreams and her imagination.

Amelia walks on stilts while Muriel plays on the swing.

She and her sister made up adventure stories about two pretend playmates, Laura and Ringa. Amelia wrote plays about adventures in far-off lands. The girls acted out these stories with their cousins. Playing with Amelia was great fun.

Amelia loved to read stories and books about nature.

Muriel

Amelia

Amy and Edwin Earhart

A family portrait: Amelia with her sister, parents, uncle, grandmother, and aunt.

Chapter 2

School Days

The Earhart family moved many times when Amelia was growing up. They moved from Kansas to Iowa. At other times, they lived in Minnesota, Missouri, and Illinois. Amelia enjoyed discovering all the new people and places.

In school, Amelia was a serious student. She did not laugh or talk in class like the other students. Amelia wanted to learn. She often sat reading in the school library because she thought she did not learn enough in class. She spent much of her time alone.

After Amelia graduated in 1916, she went to a two-year women's college near Philadelphia. She was nineteen now, and very tall and slender.

Amelia, age seventeen: In school she was a quiet girl who liked to be alone.

Amelia kept a scrapbook of newspaper clippings. She liked to save articles about women with interesting jobs. One was a bank president. Another was a fire lookout at a national park.

In those days, most women dreamed of getting married and having children. But not Amelia. She dreamed of having a career.

In 1917, Amelia went to Toronto, Canada, to visit

her sister, who was in college there. Canadian soldiers had been fighting in World War I for three years. Many soldiers were badly hurt. Some were blind; others had arms or legs missing. Amelia was horrified by what she saw. She was determined to help them.

During the summer of 1918, Amelia worked six days a week at a hospital in Toronto. Sometimes she worked fourteen hours a day. But when Amelia had free time, she enjoyed horseback riding and playing tennis. She also visited a nearby airfield. She liked watching the planes take off.

Flying was still new. It was only fifteen years since the Wright brothers' famous flight in 1903. They had invented the

Amelia helped take care of soldiers in a hospital.

The Wright brothers' airplanes amazed the world.
This picture was taken in 1911.

first airplane that flew through the air powered by an engine.

When Amelia became sick with the flu, she had to stop working at the hospital. After she got better, Amelia began studying at Columbia University in New York City. She thought about becoming a doctor.

Amelia worked hard at school. But she was still adventurous. Sometimes she climbed to the top of the library at school. From the roof, she watched the sun set on New York.

Amelia's parents had moved to California, and they invited her for a visit. Amelia was still deciding what to do with her life. She no longer wanted to become a doctor. So Amelia left school and headed out west to see her parents.

Amelia and her father went to an air show in Long Beach, California. At air shows, pilots did flying stunts for the crowds. Amelia had first seen an airplane at a country fair when she was almost eleven. She did not find it very interesting.

Amelia liked to sit on the round roof of her college library to watch the sunset.

At air shows, pilots showed off their skill with flying stunts.

But at age twenty-three, Amelia's feelings were very different. She could not take her eyes off the airplanes. She even paid money to go up in a plane for a ten-minute ride. From that moment on, Amelia knew what she wanted to do.

She told her family, "I think I'd like to learn to fly."

Chapter 3

Learning to Fly

**A**melia took flying lessons in 1921 from a woman pilot. The first few lessons were held on the ground. Amelia needed to learn how an airplane worked before she could fly one in the air. She practiced takeoffs and landings. Less than a year later, Amelia flew by herself. Soon, she earned her pilot's license.

Amelia's parents and sister worried about her.

Amelia had to learn how to use all the dials in the cockpit of her airplane.

She had already made two crash landings. One time, Amelia had to bring the plane down in a cabbage field. Another time, the plane got tangled in some trees. Luckily, Amelia was not hurt.

One day, when Amelia was twenty-five, she gave her sister and father tickets to an air show. But she did not sit with them. They wondered where she went—until they saw Amelia flying a plane high into the clouds. She soared 14,000 feet into the air. Amelia had flown higher than any woman in history!

Amelia now owned her own plane. Flying was expensive, so she worked at many jobs, such as

Pilot Neta Snook, left, taught Amelia how to fly.

driving a truck, selling sausages, and taking photographs.

But money was still in short supply. Amelia traveled to Boston and took a job helping other people. During the week, she taught English to Chinese, Syrian, and Armenian children. On the weekends, she flew.

In Amelia's day, cameras were big and heavy.

When Amelia was thirty-one, she was asked to join two pilots in a flight across the Atlantic Ocean. A year earlier, in May 1927, Charles Lindbergh had become the first man to fly alone across the ocean. Now Amelia would be the first woman to make the flight across the Atlantic Ocean.

Charles Lindbergh was the first pilot to fly solo across the ocean.

18

Chapter 4

Across the Ocean

 **A**melia did not want to cross the ocean as a passenger. She really wanted to pilot the plane. Still, she called the trip a "grand adventure." And Amelia never passed up an adventure.

The plane was named *Friendship*. It was painted bright orange. In case there was an accident, the plane would be easy to spot.

Friendship took off on June 3, 1928. The plane

started its journey in Newfoundland, Canada, heading for Great Britain. Amelia squeezed into the cabin behind Wilmer Stutz, the pilot, and Lou Gordon, the mechanic. Her job was to be the navigator—to check maps and keep track of the plane's height above the ocean.

Amelia crossed the Atlantic Ocean in a plane named *Friendship*.

Amelia also took notes about what she saw. "The sea looks like the back of an elephant," she wrote.

Friendship landed in Wales, Great Britain, on June 18. It had taken a little more than twenty hours to cross the ocean. Two thousand people came out to see the airplane. But they were mostly interested in seeing Amelia.

She was mobbed by people who wanted to

shake her hand. Reporters asked many questions. But Amelia could not understand all the excitement. After all, she was not the plane's pilot. "I was just baggage," she said.

Yet Amelia Earhart had become a hero. President Calvin Coolidge sent her a note. He praised her for being the first woman to fly across the Atlantic Ocean. When Amelia returned to New York City, the crowds cheered for her.

A publisher named George Putnam asked Amelia to write about her experience. Her book, called *20 Hrs. 40 Min.*, came out in 1929.

After their flight, Wilmer Stutz, Amelia Earhart, and Lou Gordon were treated like heroes.

GREENLAND   ICELAND

Solo flight route

Londonderry,
Ireland

GREAT BRITAIN

Burry Port,
Wales

CANADA

Harbour
Grace

Friendship route

Trepassey

EUROPE

Newfoundland

UNITED
STATES
OF
AMERICA

Atlantic
Ocean

Friendship flight in 1928
Solo flight in 1932

AFRICA

The long flight across the ocean was very dangerous.

It was a huge success. Two years later, Amelia Earhart married George Putnam.

Amelia was now traveling around the country giving lectures. She talked about world peace and the need to treat everyone fairly. She told listeners that women could have both a family and a career. She also said that fathers should play a stronger role in raising their children.

Amelia's picture was everywhere. She appeared in ads for baby food, cars, and pajamas. Americans admired her short hair, simple way of dress, and clear gray eyes.

But Amelia wanted to prove that she deserved all this attention. So shortly before her thirty-fifth birthday, in 1932, Amelia took another flight. She became the first woman in history to fly alone across the Atlantic Ocean.

Amelia and George Putnam were married in 1931.

Amelia landed in a meadow in Ireland, where cows were grazing. A farmer came over to the plane and stared.

"Have you come far?" he asked.

"From America," said Amelia with a smile.

Chapter 5

Mysterious End

**A**melia continued to break flying records. In 1935, she became the first pilot—man or woman—to fly alone over the Pacific Ocean. That same year, she also became the first person to fly solo from Los Angeles, California, to Mexico.

But there was still one thing Amelia wanted to do. She wanted to fly around the world.

Amelia got her chance on June 1, 1937. She set

out on the flight with Fred Noonan as her navigator. She planned to follow a route close to the equator.

Amelia began her journey in Miami, Florida, and headed east. Over the next month, she made stops in South America, Africa, Asia, Australia, and the island of New Guinea.

By this time, Amelia had flown two-thirds of the way around the world. She was very tired. She wanted to return home in time to celebrate two special dates: the Fourth of July and her fortieth birthday.

When Amelia left Lae, New Guinea, on July 2,

Fred and Amelia inspected their plane carefully before takeoff.

she was headed for Howland Island in the Pacific Ocean. From there, she planned to fly to Hawaii and then end her trip in California.

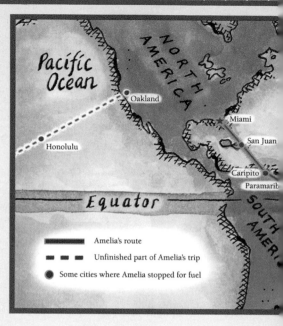

Some people came to the airfield in New Guinea to see Amelia's plane take off. They were the last people to see her alive. Amelia and Fred never made it to Howland Island. Their plane vanished somewhere over the ocean.

No one knows what happened to Amelia's plane. Most people think Amelia was not able to find the island. From the air, Howland Island would look like a tiny speck in the ocean. The day was cloudy, and Amelia may have run out of fuel as she searched for a place to land.

A U.S. Coast Guard ship had been waiting near

the island. It was to send and receive radio messages from Amelia. But Amelia had taken some of the radio equipment out of her plane to make the plane lighter. She could not receive all the messages sent by the ship.

Amelia Earhart's disappearance is still a mystery.

What happened to Amelia's plane? Many planes and ships combed the waters of the Pacific Ocean. They checked all the islands in the area.

The search lasted more than two weeks. But no trace of Amelia, Fred, or the plane was ever found.

Amelia Earhart was the most famous female pilot in the world. She devoted her life to showing that women could do anything men could do. Amelia worked hard, and she loved adventure. She knew that flying was risky. But she said, "The fun of it is worth the price."

"Pilots are always dreaming dreams," wrote Amelia before her last flight.

Timeline

1897~Born July 24 in Atchison, Kansas.

1908~Sees her first airplane at the Iowa State Fair.

1919~Enrolls at Columbia University in New York.

1921~Begins flying lessons with Neta Snook.

1922~Buys her first plane. Flies higher than any other woman pilot.

1928~Becomes the first woman to fly across the Atlantic Ocean (as a passenger).

1931~Marries George Putnam on February 7.

1932~Becomes the first woman to fly alone across the Atlantic Ocean.

1935~Becomes the first person to fly alone from Hawaii to California.

1937~Begins her flight around the world. Her plane disappears on July 2.

Words to Know

air show—An exhibit of airplanes, with pilots performing daring tricks in the air.

equator—An imaginary line around the middle of the earth. It divides the globe into two halves—north and south.

navigator—A person who maps the route for a plane or boat to travel.

pilot's license—A paper saying that a person is legally allowed to fly a plane.

publisher—A person or company that makes books.

U.S. Coast Guard—Soldiers who make sure the coastline is safe and that boats obey the laws.

World War I—A war fought in Europe, Asia, and Africa from 1914 to 1918.

Wright brothers—The two men who, in 1903, flew the first airplane with an engine.

Books

David A. Adler. *A Picture Book of Amelia Earhart.* New York: Holiday House, 1999.

Francene Sabin. *Amelia Earhart: Adventure in the Sky.* New York: Troll Communications, 1989.

Corrine Szabo. *Sky Pioneer: A Photobiography of Amelia Earhart.* Washington, D.C.: National Geographic Society, 1997.

Internet Addresses

Amelia Earhart Birthplace Museum
<http://www.ameliaearhartmuseum.org/index.html>

Meet Amazing Americans: Amelia Earhart
<http://www.americaslibrary.gov/cgi-bin/page.cgi/aa/earhart>

The official Amelia Earhart Web Site Photo Gallery
<http://www.ameliaearhart.com/photo.html>

Index